go Steel

Pittsburgh Steelers
Coloring & Activity Storybook

by Brad M. Epstein
illustrations by Curt Walstead

michaelson entertainment

Aliso Viejo, CA www.michaelsonentertainment.com
Designed in California

National Football League Coloring & Activity Books
Copyright ©2015 Michaelson Entertainment, All Rights Reserved
Official Publication of the National Football League

ISBN-13: 978-1-60730-524-8

Thousands of Pittsburgh Steelers fans are arriving at

Heinz Field for the big game.

The Steelers players are getting ready in the locker room.

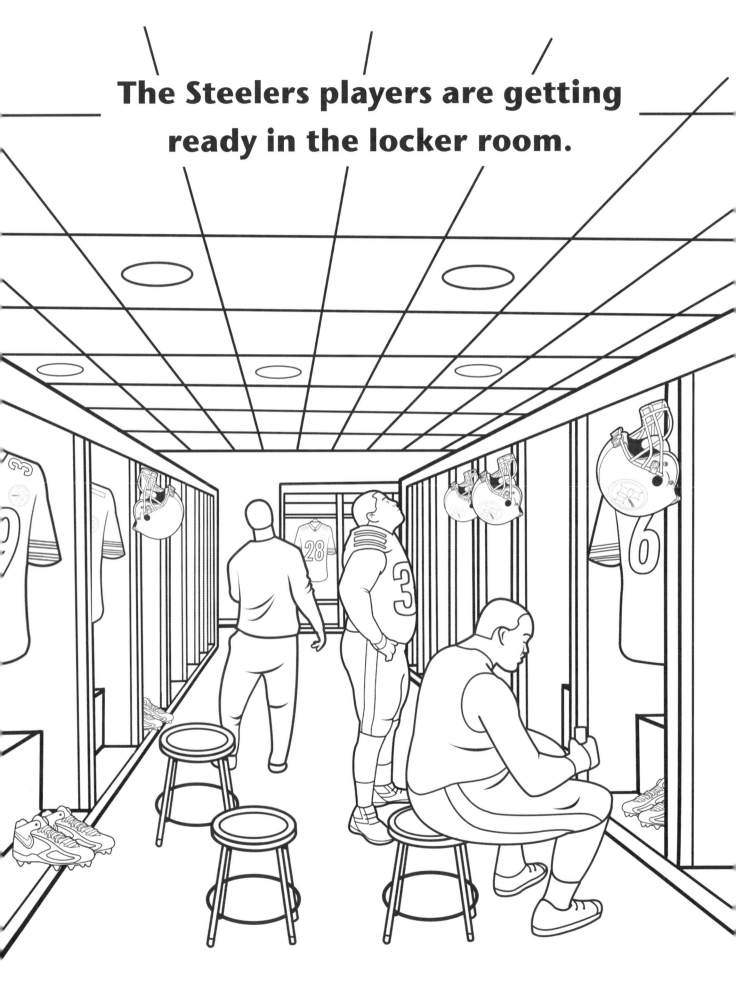

Help the players get into their

uniforms.

Unscramble the words.

e l h t e m

_____

r j y e s e

_____

v l o e s g

_____

e e n k   s p a d

_____ _____

c t s e a l

_____

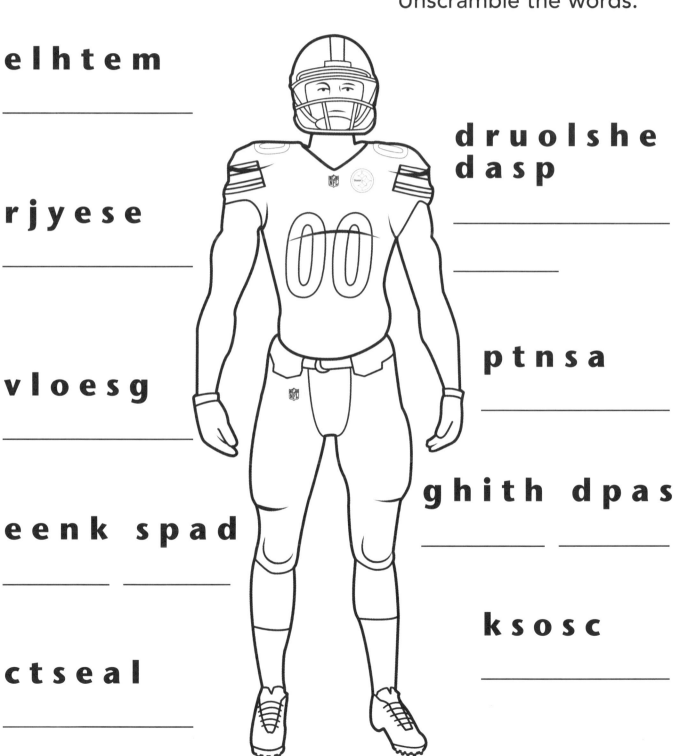

d r u o l s h e
d a s p

_____

p t n s a

_____

g h i t h   d p a s

_____ _____

k s o s c

_____

The Steelers take the field!

Here's a close-up of the **Steelers** **jersey**

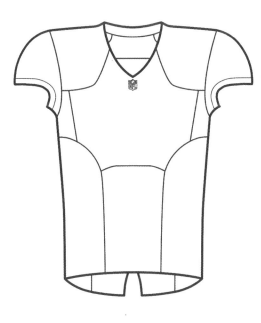

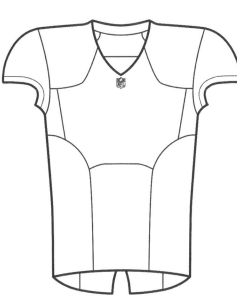

Color it in,
then create your own jersey designs.

kickoff

Our
kicker
kicks the ball.

the Steelers are awesome!

```
S  T  D  E  F  E  N  S  E  N  G  Z
U  T  L  S  G  X  B  D  V  I  X  A
P  H  E  T  K  C  A  L  B  A  H  T
E  G  I  E  F  M  E  O  K  T  E  O
R  R  F  N  L  W  A  G  O  R  X  X
B  U  Z  J  O  Y  X  F  R  U  L  L
O  B  N  T  R  I  M  I  C  C  P  I
W  S  I  U  I  D  B  C  A  L  Z  I
L  T  E  I  M  L  F  N  B  E  O  I
O  T  H  R  E  E  R  I  V  E  R  S
P  I  T  T  S  B  U  R  G  T  A  W
Y  P  S  R  E  L  E  E  T  S  O  M
```

Word Search:
Find the Pittsburgh Steelers football words in this list.

Black	**Pittsburgh**	**Super Bowl**
Defense	**Steel Curtain**	**Terrible**
Gold	**Steelers**	**Three Rivers**
Heinz Field	**Steely McBeam**	**Towel**

timeout: find the Steelers Super Bowl championships (IX, X, XIII, XIV, XL, XLIII)

The Steelers **offense** is on the field. It's first and ten at the twenty yard line.

The

quarterback

fades back to pass.

Help the Steelers quarterback throw a
complete pass.

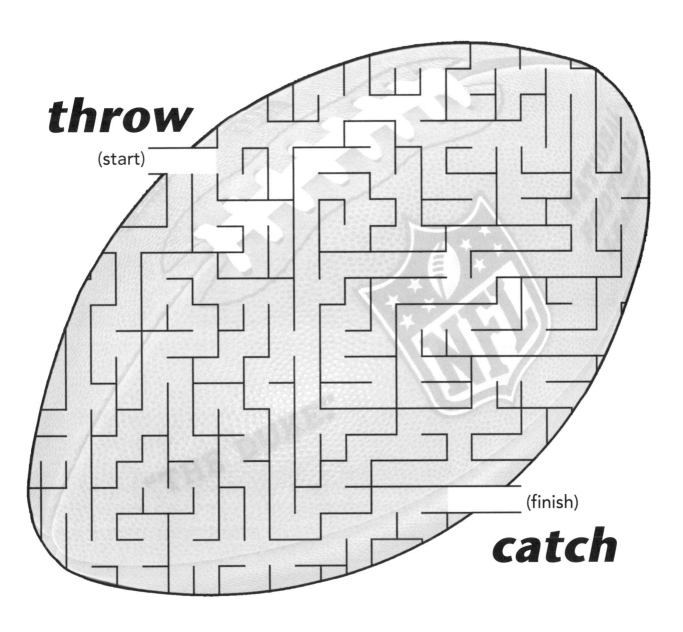

throw
(start)

(finish)
catch

Find a path from the quarterback's
throw to the wide receiver's catch.

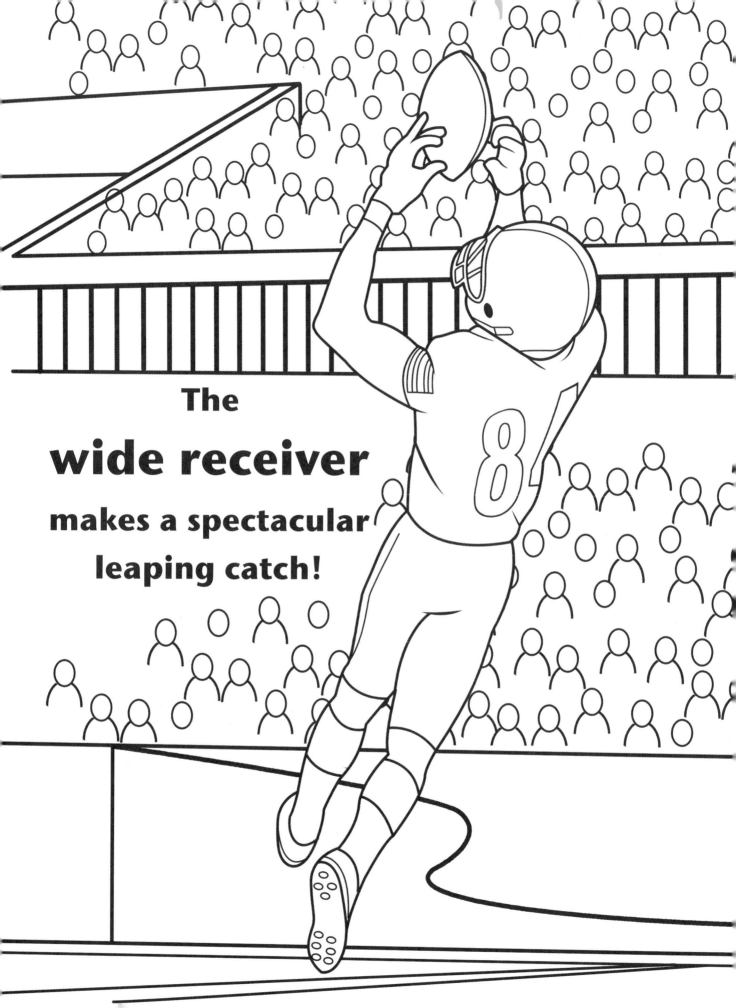

The **wide receiver** makes a spectacular leaping catch!

Everyone is cheering.

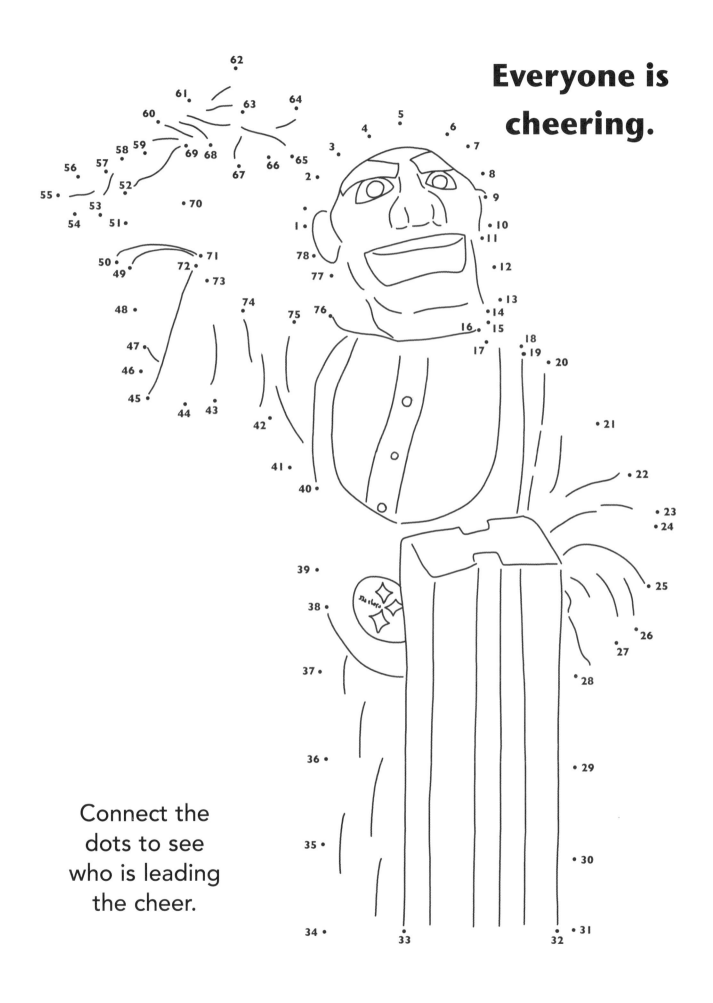

Connect the
dots to see
who is leading
the cheer.

It's 2nd down. Make sure the players are in their correct positions.

```
N C E N T E R R A H S W
G U O Z O Y T E F A S E
U T R R O R E T D L A C
A V E E N L M N Q F P O
R E K S E E U U B R Z
D A C C N L R P V A E O
Q U A R T E R B A C K H
A T B T O O F X A K C H
N R E V I E C E R C I C
E S N E F F O Q D A K A
O D I Z M A N A G E R O
C A L K C A B L L U F C
```

Word Search: Find the names of the players and their positions in this list.

Cornerback	Guard	Punter
Center	Halfback	Quarterback
Defense	Kicker	Receiver
End	Linebacker	Safety
Fullback	Offense	Tackle

Huddle Up

It's a handoff, and...

...the Steelers star **running back** breaks a tackle... and runs into the end zone!

TOUCHDOWN!

How many points are earned for each scoring play?

Unscramble the words, then match the scoring play to the correct number of points.

fastye

_____

2

eaxrt ipotn

_____ _____

6

chodtuwno

_____

3

fleid loag

_____ _____

1

Instant Replay!

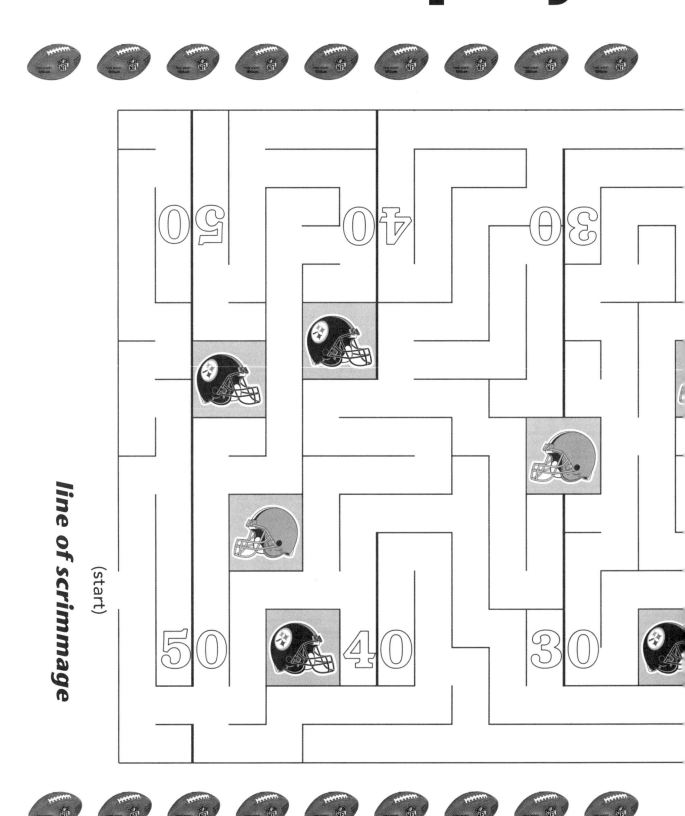

line of scrimmage

(start)

Let's see how the running back scored the touchdown.
Find a path from the line of scrimmage to the end zone.
(don't get 'tackled' by the Cleveland Browns helmets)

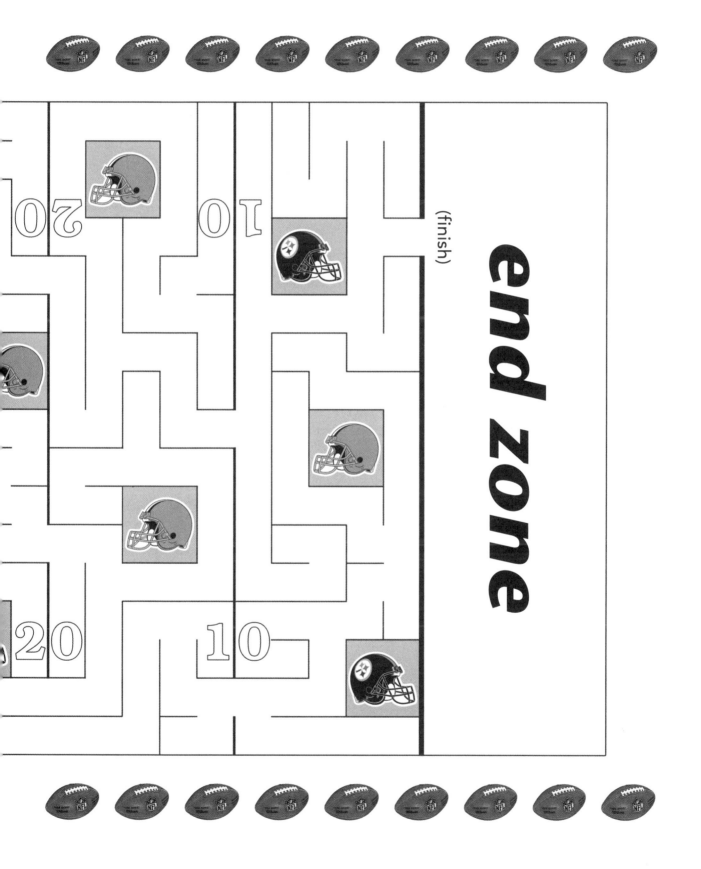

All of the **Pittsburgh Steelers**

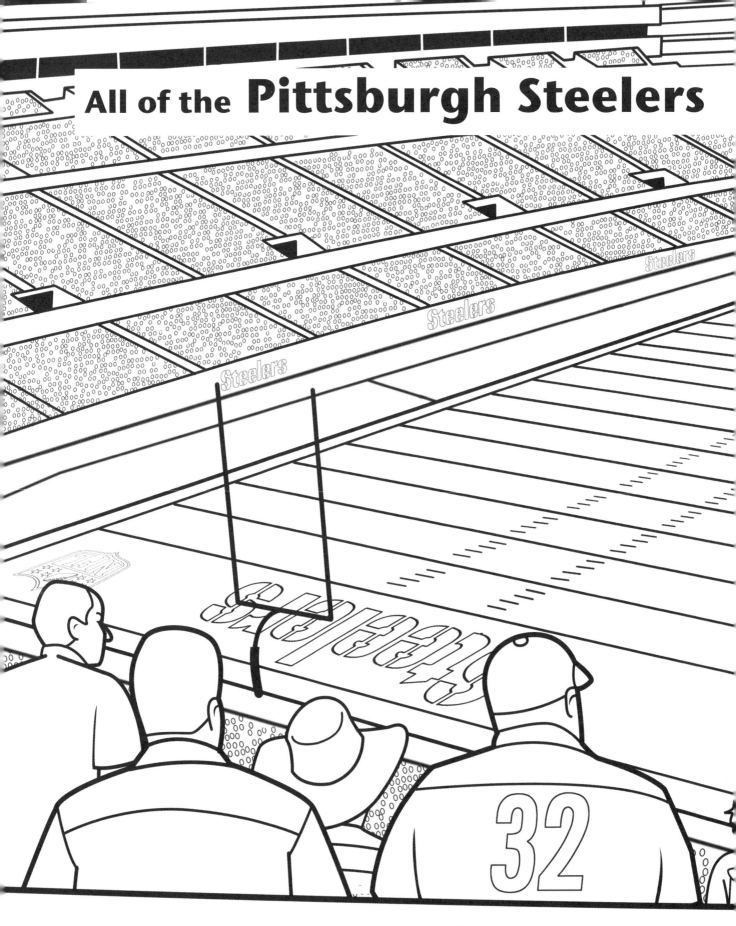

Color in the stadium, draw some fans too.

fans are on their feet,

cheering in **Heinz Field.**

Let's put a **Steelers logo**
on the 50-yard line of the field.

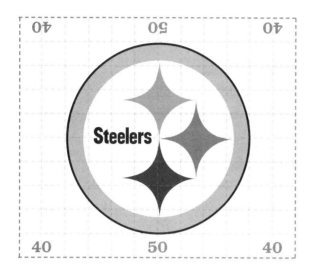

Use the grid as a guide to draw a big Pittsburgh Steelers logo on the 'field' below. We've started with the top left corner.

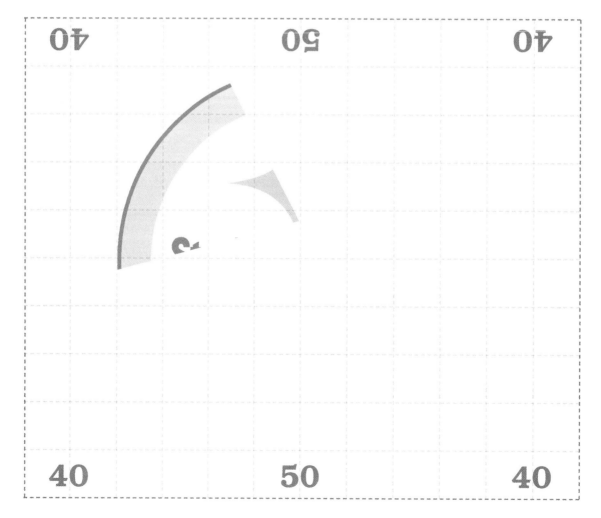

it's halftime

What does every Steelers fan know? Solve the message by using the secret code below.

_T_ _H_ _E_

_S_ _T_ _E_ _E_ _L_ _E_ _R_ _S_

_A_

_A_ _R_ _E_   _T_ _H_ _E_

_G_ _R_ _E_ _A_ _T_ _E_ _S_ _T_

= A		= H		= S	
= E		= L		= T	
= G		= R			

enter the

color in the Steelers
megacore

Help protect the home team in the Rush Zone!

```
I  P  T  E  L  A  N  G  P  D  O  T
M  E  G  A  C  O  R  E  D  R  E  C
L  R  R  R  T  E  A  M  L  A  N  D
U  F  S  N  W  O  L  A  T  C  M  W
L  L  A  B  T  O  O  F  R  D  W  N
I  C  H  R  H  A  A  F  R  L  H  D
L  B  L  I  T  Z  B  O  T  I  S  Z
E  B  O  S  M  N  P  L  Q  W  U  O
N  M  Z  H  D  K  E  L  H  R  R  N
K  F  N  A  I  D  R  A  U  G  I  E
R  A  L  C  O  R  E  H  S  U  R  E
O  K  K  H  M  R  M  I  R  S  A  K
```

Word Search: Find the names of
these things in the Rush Zone.

Blitz Bot	**Guardian**	**Ohio**
Canton	**Hall of Fame**	**Rusher**
Drop Kick	**Ish**	**Teamland**
Football	**Megacore**	**Wild Card**

Watch out for
imposters!

Can you find the
10 differences
between the real
Steelers Rusher
on the top and
the imposter on
the bottom?

Steelers Rusher

The 2nd half is about to start.

Make some noise!

Color in the Steelers logo

The **center** snaps
the ball to start
the play...

Steely McBeam

is on the sideline, cheering for our team!

great
tackle

Our
defense
is on
the field.

Play by Play

It is a close game but our team is behind by 2 points.
You are the coach. Can you tell our players what to do?
(circle the correct answers)

Our **coach**/**defense**/**offense** needs to stop the Browns' offense.

....

Then we need to recover a **fumble**/**tackle**/**touchdown** or we need to

force an **interception**/**pass**/**penalty** to take possession.

....

Our offense will need to score at least **two**/**three**/**four** points to take the lead.

....

We need to score a **extra point**/**field goal**/**first down** or a **block**/**punt**/**touchdown** to win.

It's 4th down, we need a **field goal** to win the game.

It's long enough, it's good.

SCORE!

Instant Replay!

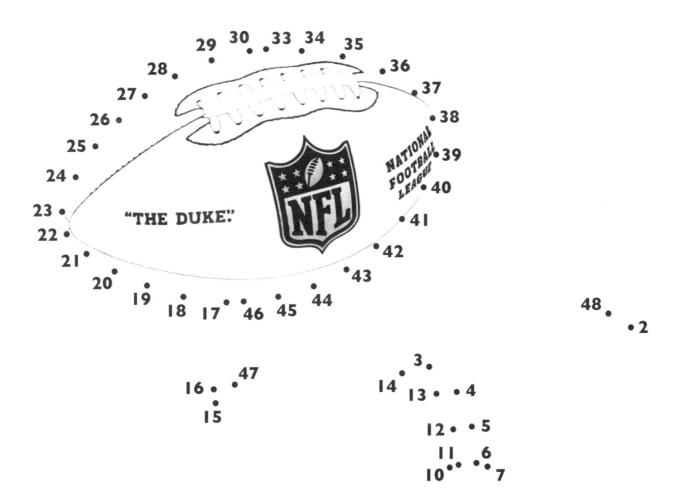

Connect the dots to see a
close-up of the field goal.

The Steelers win!

What is the goal of every player? Solve the message by using the secret code below.

 = A    = I    = P    = U

 = B   = L   = R   = W

= E   = N   = S   = Y

 = H   = O   = T

If the Steelers are the best team, we can

_____

It will be difficult because
There are 32 awesome teams

Bengals _____

Bills ___a___

Broncos _____

Browns _____

Chargers _____

Chiefs _____

Colts _____

Dolphins _____

Jaguars _____

Jets _____

Patriots _____

Raiders _____

Ravens _____

Steelers _____

Texans _____

Titans _____

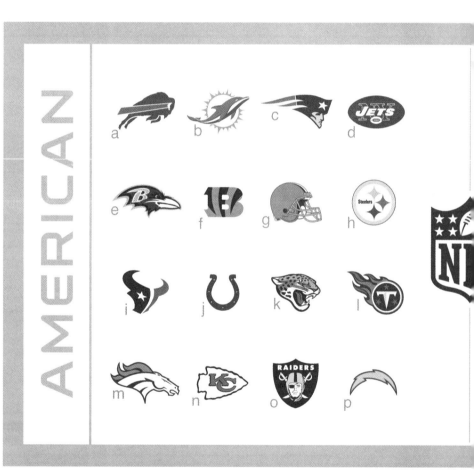

Match each te⋯
(example⋯

win the Super Bowl.

ere is a lot of competition.
the National Football League.

NATIONAL

Bears _____

Buccaneers _____

Cardinals _____

Cowboys _____

Eagles _____

Falcons _____

Forty Niners _____

Giants _____

Lions _____

Packers _____

Panthers _____

Rams _____

Redskins _____

Saints _____

Seahawks _____

Vikings _____

with its logo.

ills is 'a')

The game is over. It's time to go home.

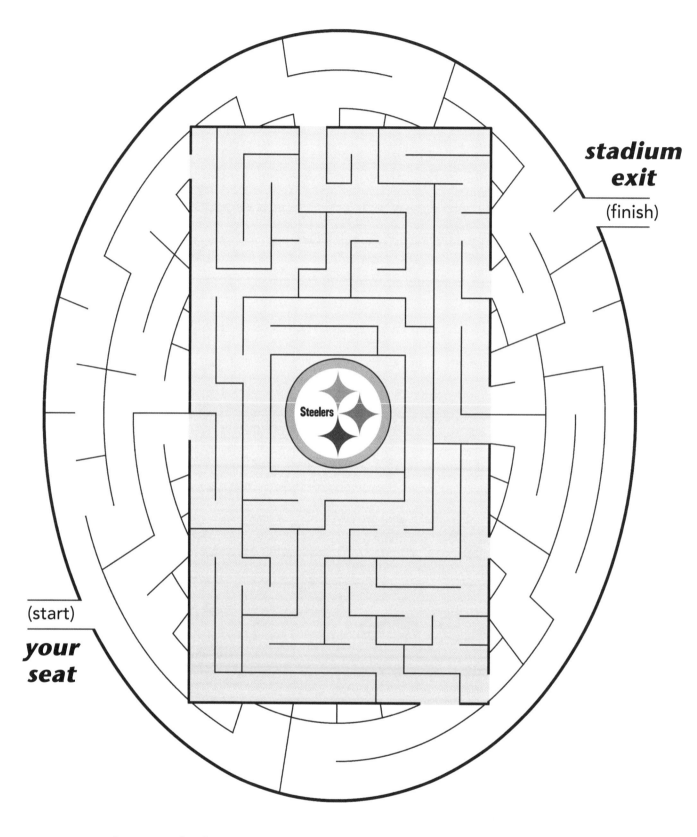

stadium exit
(finish)

(start)
your seat

Find a path from 'your seat' to the 'stadium exit.'

Let's draw the NFL logo.

Use the grid as a
guide to draw a
big NFL logo.
We've started with
the top left corner.

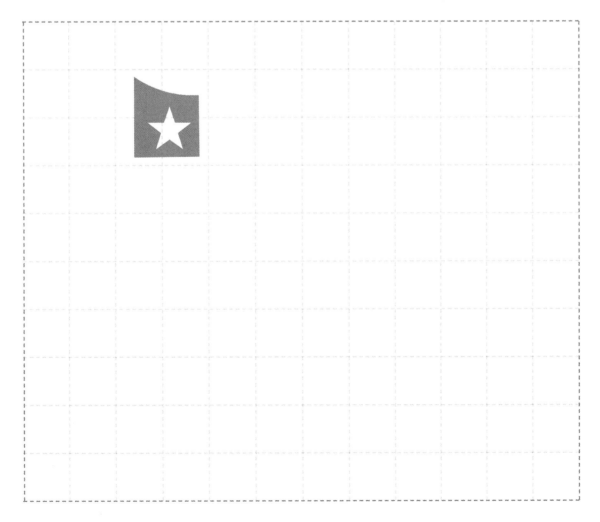

Solutions to Games and Puzzles

Page 5

Help the players get into their
uniforms.
Unscramble the words.

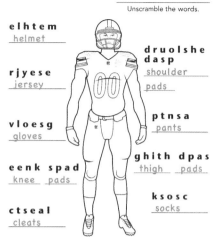

elhtem
helmet

rjyese
jersey

vloesg
gloves

eenk spad
knee   pads

ctseal
cleats

druolshe dasp
shoulder   pads

ptnsa
pants

ghith dpas
thigh   pads

ksosc
socks

Page 11

the Steelers are awesome!

Word Search:
Find the Pittsburgh Steelers football words in this list.

Black	Pittsburgh	Super Bowl
Defense	Steel Curtain	Terrible
Gold	Steelers	Three Rivers
Heinz Field	Steely McBeam	Towel

timeout: find the Steelers Super Bowl championships (IX, X, XIII, XIV, XL, XLIII)

Page 15

Help the Steelers quarterback throw a
complete pass.

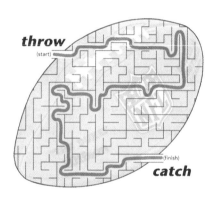

throw (start)

catch (finish)

Find a path from the quarterback's
throw to the wide receiver's catch.

Page 17

Everyone is cheering.

Connect the
dots to see
who is leading
the cheer.

Page 18

**It's 2nd down. Make sure the players
are in their correct positions.**

Word Search: Find the names of the
players and their positions in this list.

Cornerback	Guard	Punter
Center	Halfback	Quarterback
Defense	Kicker	Receiver
End	Linebacker	Safety
Fullback	Offense	Tackle

Page 21

TOUCHDOWN!
**How many points are
earned for each scoring play?**

Unscramble the words, then
match the scoring play to the
correct number of points.

fastye
safety — **2**

eaxrt ipotn
extra   point — **6**

chodtuwno
touchdown — **3**

fleid loag
field   goal — **1**